CITIES OF THE WORLD

JERUSALEM

BY DEBORAH KENT

CHILDREN'S PRESS®
A Division of Scholastic Inc.
New York Toronto London Auckland Sydney
Mexico City New Delhi Hong Kong
Danbury, Connecticut

CONSULTANTS

Carl W. Ernst, Ph.D.
Zachary Smith Professor, Department of Religious Studies
University of North Carolina
Chapel Hill, North Carolina

Linda Cornwell
Coordinator of School Quality and Professional Improvement
Indiana State Teachers Association

Project Editor: Downing Publishing Services
Design Director: Karen Kohn & Associates; J. Breslin
Photo Researcher: Jan Izzo
Pronunciations: Courtesy of Dalia Hoffman, MA, Medieval English Literature; Jamil Khoury, Cross-Cultural Trainer, MA, Religious Studies, University of Chicago; and Tony Breed, M.A., Linguistics, University of Chicago

---

NOTES ON PRONUNCIATION

Most of the Hebrew pronunciations in this book are based on current Israeli pronunciation. Traditional Ashkenazi pronunciation, often heard in the United States, is sometimes different. Most pronunciations are exactly as they look, with the following notes: *ghee* is like the *gea* in gear; *oo* is as in food; <u>h</u> is like the *h* in hat but stonger and harsher. If you try to say *k* as in kite but relax and slur the sound, it will sound like *h*.

Library of Congress Cataloging-in-Publication Data
Kent, Deborah
    Jerusalem / by Deborah Kent.
      p. cm. — (Cities of the world)
Includes bibliographical references and index.
Summary: Describes the history, culture, daily life, food, people, sports, and points of interest in the capital of Israel.
    ISBN 0-516-22241-4 (lib. bdg.)   0-516-25960-1 (pbk.)
    1. Jerusalem—Juvenile literature. [1. Jerusalem] I. Title.
II. Series:
DS109.15.K46 2001
956.94'42—dc21   00-060123

TABLE OF CONTENTS

Eight stone staircases rise to the crown of Temple Mount in the city of Jerusalem. Over the centuries, countless feet have worn deep furrows into the steps. Visitors must climb slowly, gingerly, up the uneven stones. At the top, they reach the Dome of the Rock, one of Jerusalem's most beautiful buildings.

Many of the visitors who make their way to the Dome of the Rock are ordinary tourists, eager to see Jerusalem's famous sights. But many more are religious pilgrims. They journey to this special place as an expression of their faith. Temple Mount is honored by followers of three of the world's great religions—Judaism, Christianity, and Islam.

Within the Dome of the Rock stands a massive stone. According to ancient teachings, God once commanded the prophet Abraham to sacrifice his son upon this rock. At the last moment, God halted Abraham and spared the boy's life. A version of the story appears in the Koran, the holy book of Islam. A somewhat similar story is told in the Torah, a body of religious writings central to the Jewish faith. The Torah consists of the first five books of the Old Testament of the Holy Bible. The Old Testament is sacred to both Jews and Christians. Abraham is considered a patriarch, or founding father, of all three faiths.

Jerusalem is a holy city to Jews, Christians, and Muslims (members of the Islamic community). The city contains numerous sites that are holy to one or more of these traditions. Despite this deep religious meaning, Jerusalem has

The Dome of the Rock, one of the most beautiful buildings in Jerusalem

*Orthodox
children
playing
in the
Old City*

been embattled ground throughout its long history. Over the centuries, it has been conquered by members of one faith, then claimed by followers of another. Time after time, the streets of this holy city have been darkened with blood. It is ironic that the name *Jerusalem* comes from words that mean "city of peace."

Today, Jerusalem is governed by the Jewish nation of Israel. Since its founding in 1948, Israel has been locked in conflict with neighboring Arab nations. Rights to the land lie at the heart of this long-standing conflict.

Jews, Christians, and Muslims are the dominant groups in Jerusalem. Year by year, the people of this

*A Muslim man
of Jerusalem*

unique city struggle toward mutual understanding. Year by year, they strive to make Jerusalem a city of peace in truth as well as in name.

"The air over Jerusalem is saturated with prayers and dreams," writes Israeli poet Yehudah Amichai. "It's hard to breathe." The prayers and dreams are launched by Jews, Christians, and Muslims, the people who call Jerusalem their home. In some ways, the beliefs and longings of these three groups overlap. In other ways, they are radically different. Jerusalem, the holy city of three faiths, is torn by deep divisions.

THE CITY IN THE HILLS

Jerusalem is built on a series of hills. In some places, the streets are so steep that the sidewalks are stairways. Most of the city's buildings are made of local stone that is pink, beige, or cream in tone. The stone facades and the hilltop views make Jerusalem one of the loveliest cities on earth.

Above: Israel's Dead Sea is the lowest place on earth.
Left: An aerial view of Jerusalem

Summer days in Jerusalem are dry and intensely hot. At sundown, the temperature drops, and the nights are comfortably cool. Even during the winter months, the climate is relatively mild. Snowfall is virtually unknown, and rainfall is light. Much of the land around Jerusalem is desert. To the south and east lies a body of extremely salty water known as the Dead Sea.

Visitors to the Ein Gedi Health Spa on the shore of the Dead Sea can take hot sulfur baths.

Mud soap and bath salts from the Dead Sea are sold at many shops and spas in Jerusalem and its surrounding areas.

The city of Jerusalem is located in central Israel, pressed against the border of the neighboring nation of Jordan. With 567,000 people, it is about the size of the United States city of Seattle. The city is divided into two sections, East Jerusalem and West Jerusalem. West Jerusalem largely developed after 1947. It is a bustling, modern city with businesses, factories, and fancy hotels. Shopping malls display the latest fashions from Europe and the United States, and cinemas show first-run movies. Traffic speeds along a network of superhighways.

East Jerusalem, on the other hand, clings to its traditions. Open-air markets offer fruits and vegetables fresh from the countryside. Craftspeople in tiny workshops make pottery, baskets, jewelry, furniture, and leather goods. Many streets are so narrow that automobile traffic is impossible. Donkeys and camels carry passengers and bundles, as they have for thousands of years.

Israeli (IZ-RAY-LEE)

A wooden camel from a Jerusalem souvenir shop

Camels and donkeys are often used for transportation in East Jerusalem.

East Jerusalem is about twice the size of West Jerusalem, but it has only three-fourths the number of people. West Jerusalem is mainly Jewish, while most of the people in East Jerusalem are Christian or Muslim Arabs. For nineteen years, from 1948 until 1967, the city was actually split by a political boundary. West Jerusalem lay within Israeli borders, while Jordan controlled East Jerusalem. Israel captured East Jerusalem during a war in June of 1967. Jerusalem is now united under a single government, but it continues to function as two cities in one.

THE THREE HOLY DAYS

Al Aqsa (AH-LOK-SAH)

According to Islamic tradition, Friday is a day of prayer. In Jerusalem's Muslim neighborhoods, shops close on Friday afternoons. Men and women kneel in prayer at their local mosques, or visit the magnificent mosque called Al-Aqsa on Temple Mount.

Saturday is the Sabbath according to the Jewish calendar. Orthodox, or traditional, Jews do not work, conduct business, or cook food between sundown on Friday and sundown on Saturday. Families attend services at their local synagogue and gather for a meal that was carefully prepared the day before.

In Jerusalem's Christian communities, church bells ring out every Sunday. The city's Christians are members of many denominations. Jerusalem has Lutheran, Roman Catholic, Greek Orthodox, Russian Orthodox, and several other Christian churches.

Two rabbis, Jewish religious leaders

Three Christmases

Not only do Jerusalemites honor three Sabbaths, Christian groups in the city celebrate three different Christmases. Protestants and Roman Catholics celebrate Christmas on December 25. January 7 is Christmas according to the Greek and Syrian Orthodox calendars. Armenian Orthodox Christians celebrate Christmas on January 19.

A hand-blown ornament with the city of Jerusalem painted on it

An Orthodox priest at the Church of the Holy Sepulchre in Jerusalem, which was built on what is believed to be the site of Christ's crucifixion

About 83 percent of all Jerusalem's people are Jewish. More than half the city's Jews emigrated to Israel after its founding as a nation in 1948. Among these immigrants are Sephardic Jews, whose ancestors lived in Spain and Portugal, and Ashkenazi Jews, who have roots in eastern Europe. Jews who lived here before Israel was established as a nation are known as *sabras*.

Jerusalem's Jewish community is subdivided in other ways as well. Jews in the city fall into three groups—secular, Orthodox, and Ultra Orthodox.

Secular Jews are divided into two groups, Reformed and Conservative. Most secular Jews are immigrants from the United States and western Europe. They feel a strong connection with Jewish history and culture, but they do not follow the strict religious laws of their faith. Secular Jews hold considerable power in the government and run many of Jerusalem's businesses.

Sephardic (SEH-FAR-DIK)
Ashkenazi (OSH-KEH-NAH-ZEE)
sabra (SAH-BRAH)

Among Jerusalem's Orthodox Jews are the Ashkenazi from eastern Europe and the Oriental Jews from parts of Africa and the Middle East. Orthodox Jews are careful to follow the rules set down in the Torah. They are strict in observing the Sabbath. They also keep kosher, observing a set of rules concerning food and its preparation. Kosher meat comes from animals that have been slaughtered under the supervision of a rabbi, or religious leader. Orthodox Jews dress conservatively. Women wear black dresses and black stockings. Men wear long black coats and dangling side curls, or earlocks. Despite the warm climate, Orthodox men sometimes wear fur-trimmed hats like those their ancestors wore in Russia.

About 30 percent of Jerusalem's Jews are Ultra Orthodox. This group is the strictest of all in dress and customs. An Ultra-Orthodox woman is not permitted to be in a room with a man other than her husband or a relative. After she marries, she must shave her head and wear a wig as a sign of humility. Ultra-Orthodox Jews do not drive cars on the Sabbath, and would like to see the city's roads closed to all traffic on that day.

The Arab community in Jerusalem is also divided. About 80 percent of the city's Arabs are Muslims, while the rest belong to various Christian churches. Most Arab men wear Western-style clothing. Some Muslim women wear veils over their faces when they go out

A street scene in Mea Shearim, a district of Jerusalem in which Ultra-Orthodox Jews live

An Arab man wearing a traditional head cloth speaks with an Arab man in Western dress.

A fabric headdress called a kaffiyeh (above) is worn by many Arab men in Jerusalem.

in public. Like Jerusalem's Jewish population, the city's Muslims are divided into several subgroups. These groups range from secular to conservative and fundamentalist. Secular Muslims have adopted scientific perspectives and socialist political views. Conservative Muslims follow traditional practices including prayer, fasting, and reverence for prophets. Fundamentalist Muslims (such as the Hamas group) use authoritarian interpretations of the Koran to oppose modern secularism and the Israeli state.

Every year on Good Friday, thousands of Christians flock to the Church of the Holy Sepulchre in East Jerusalem. The church is a magnet for visitors as well as a focus for the city's Christian population. Non-Arab Christians comprise less than 10 percent of all Jerusalem's people. Priests, nuns, and monks from various denominations walk the streets in their traditional religious clothing.

LIVING DAY TO DAY

Jerusalem draws visitors from all over the world. But it is also home to more than half a million people. What is it like to live in this fascinating city on a day-to-day basis? The answer depends very much on which part of the city you happen to call home.

West Jerusalem is a prosperous modern metropolis. Most people live in single-family homes or in modern apartments with television sets, computers, and access to the Internet. Some West Jerusalemites work in offices in high-rise buildings downtown. Others hold jobs in factories that churn out plastics, chemicals, clothing, and machinery.

Many languages are spoken on the streets of West Jerusalem. You are likely to hear Hebrew, the national language of Israel, most often. In the park or on the bus, you will also overhear conversations in English, German, Russian, and Arabic. One frequently spoken language is Yiddish, a blend of Hebrew, German, Russian, and various Eastern European languages.

An evening view of West Jerusalem

An Arab man and a Western couple atop Temple Mount

All of these languages are spoken in East Jerusalem as well as in West Jerusalem. But the main language in this part of the city is Arabic. Though increasing numbers of Jews move into East Jerusalem each year, the Arab presence remains strong. Five times a day, a trumpetlike voice rings out from the mosques, reminding Muslims to stop where they are and pray.

The division between East and West Jerusalem is a deep and painful one. Power and resources are concentrated in the western part of the city. Many East Jerusalemites work in the West, returning at night to near-poverty at home. People from East Jerusalem complain that they pay high taxes but receive few services. Schools, roads, and sanitation are generally better in the West. As recently as the 1980s, many sections of East Jerusalem did not even have electricity or running water. Arabs in East Jerusalem often say that their wishes are not heard and their needs are not met. People in West Jerusalem argue that people in East Jerusalem refuse to work toward the good of the city and the nation as a whole.

The bitterness between Jews and Arabs in Jerusalem has tangled roots. To understand today's divided city, it is necessary to look back at Jerusalem's long and troubled history.

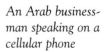

An Arab businessman speaking on a cellular phone

"NEXT YEAR IN JERUSALEM!"

Passover is one of the most important holidays in the Jewish calendar. Families gather to feast, sing, celebrate, and remember. As they say good-bye, friends and relatives often promise to share the holiday "next year in Jerusalem!"

For centuries, Jews around the world felt that Jerusalem was the heart of a homeland from which they had been cast out. Jerusalem is also a holy city for Muslims and Christians, and these groups, too, have felt painfully displaced. The history of Jerusalem is a story of strife. Each religious group has struggled for possession of this beloved holy city.

THE CITY OF DAVID

The site of present-day Jerusalem was first settled about 4,000 years ago by wandering desert tribes. Among the groups that came and went in the area were the Jebusites, the Hittites, and the Amorites. These tribes worshiped many gods. One of the Amorite deities was called Shalem, a name meaning "peace." The name "Jerusalem" comcs from the Amorite words *shalem* and *yera*. Yera meant "city." Thus, Jerusalem received its name, "City of Peace."

Jebusite (JEB-YOO-SITE)
Hittite (HIH-TITE)
Amorite (AM-UH-RITE)
Shalem (SHAH-LAME)
yera (YEH-RAH)

David, King of Israel (seated), with his son and successor, Solomon

Sometime around 1500 B.C., several new tribes migrated into the hills north of the Dead Sea. According to accounts in the Old Testament, there were twelve of these Jewish tribes, all recently freed from slavery in Egypt. In about 1000 B.C., a powerful Jewish king, David, united the tribes and established Jerusalem as his capital. The city had no harbor or river to encourage trade. But it was surrounded by hills on three sides and could be strongly defended from enemy attack. In the Old and New Testaments of the Bible, Jerusalem is often called the City of David.

In 953 B.C., King David's son, Solomon, completed construction of a temple on Jerusalem's Mount Moriah. According to the Old Testament book of 2 Chronicles, "He adorned the house with precious stones for decoration . . . he covered the whole house with gold, its rafters and frames, its walls and doors; and he carved cherubim [angels] on the walls." This splendid temple housed the Ark of the Covenant, the most sacred object the Jews had carried with them on their wanderings. Mount Moriah is commonly referred to as the Temple Mount.

Solomon's Temple

The Ark of the Covenant

On their journey out of Egypt, the Jewish tribes carried a precious gold-plated chest called the Ark of the Covenant. The Ark contained tablets inscribed with laws for the Jewish people. According to the Bible, God gave these tablets to the prophet Moses. Solomon built his temple to house the Ark of the Covenant. No one knows what became of the Ark after the temple was destroyed.

Following Solomon's death, ten of the twelve tribes broke away and formed the Kingdom of Israel. The two remaining tribes kept Jerusalem as the capital of their kingdom, which was called Judah or Judea. Judah was constantly at war with Israel and other nearby kingdoms. One king of Judah, Hezekiah, ordered his people to build a high stone wall around Jerusalem to protect it from assault. He also dug a 1,600-foot (488-meter) tunnel to pipe water into the city from the nearby Gihon Springs.

Despite the wall, Babylonian king Nebuchadnezzar conquered Jerusalem in 586 B.C. He burned Solomon's temple and killed or exiled the people of the city. Forty years later, the Persians overthrew the Babylonians and welcomed the exiles back. Persian king Cyrus helped the people of Jerusalem rebuild the temple that had been destroyed. The Second Temple, as it is called, was finished around 515 B.C.

In 586 B.C., Babylonian king Nebuchadnezzar burned Solomon's Temple and killed or exiled the people of the city.

Over the centuries, one invading army after another captured Jerusalem. The city fell into the hands of the Macedonians, the Egyptians, and the Syrians. In 186 B.C., Syrian king Antiochus IV turned the rebuilt temple into a shrine to the Greek god Zeus. The Jews staged a revolt and recaptured the temple in 154 B.C. A small group of Jews held the temple, waiting for reinforcements. According to legend, there was only enough oil to keep their lamps burning for one night. By a miracle, the oil lasted until help arrived eight nights later. This legend is the basis for the Jewish holiday of Hanukkah, the Festival of Lights, celebrated each December. For eight days, Jews the world over light candles in a special candelabra called a menorah.

This Jewish family has lit a candle in their menorah during Hannukah, the Festival of Lights.

Next, Jerusalem and the land of Judea became part of the mighty Roman Empire. During the centuries of Roman rule, the city was called Aelia Capitolina. Also during that time, a child was born to humble parents in the nearby village of Bethlehem. His birth marks the beginning of the Christian calendar that is used throughout much of the world today.

A Hanukkah candle

A menorah like this is used by Jews for the celebration of Hanukkah.

THE HEART OF CHRISTENDOM

Sometime in about the year A.D. 30, Jerusalem's Roman governor, Pontius Pilate, heard disturbing news. Crowds were turning out to hear the preachings of a man they called Jesus Christ. Jesus had little respect for Roman authority. He told the people to put God's laws before everything else. Perhaps he planned to lead a Jewish uprising. In A.D. 33, Pilate placed Jesus under arrest. He condemned Jesus to die by crucifixion, being nailed to a wooden cross. Crucifixion was a widely used form of execution in Roman times.

Following the death of Jesus, tensions continued to mount between the Jews and Romans in Jerusalem. In A.D. 70, the Romans burned the temple that the Persians had helped to rebuild. Nothing but its western wall survived the flames. The Romans set the temple ablaze on the ninth day of the Jewish month of Av, the anniversary of the day Solomon's temple burned long ago.

Roman governor Pontius Pilate sentencing Jesus Christ to death by crucifixion

After the execution of Jesus, the Romans outlawed the practice of Christianity. Worshiping in secret, Jesus' followers continued to spread their prophet's teachings. Gradually, Christianity extended throughout the Roman Empire. Around A.D. 300, Roman emperor Constantine I legalized Christianity and adopted the new religion himself. In 326, Constantine sent his mother, Queen Helena, to Judea to search for sites related to Jesus' life and death. Beneath a Roman temple, Helena discovered a crypt and three wooden crosses. She was convinced that she had found the cross on which Jesus died and the tomb where he was buried. Constantine ordered a Christian church to be built on the sacred spot. Jerusalem was now the holy city of Christendom, or the Christian world.

Eventually, the Roman Empire weakened and split in two. The strongly Christian Eastern, or Byzantine, Empire controlled Judea and the city of Jerusalem.

Above: A statue of Roman emperor Constantine I, the man who legalized Christianity around A.D. 300

Left: A fresco by Piero della Francesca called The Verification of the True Cross, *depicts the cross on which Jesus died.*

Jerusalem was not destined to remain in Christian hands for long. In about 570, a new prophet was born in far-away Arabia. He received revelations and began to preach the worship of the one true God, the God of Adam, Abraham, Moses, and Jesus. One night, the legend runs, Muhammad mounted a supernatural steed called al-Buraq. Al-Buraq had the wings of an eagle and the face of a beautiful woman. The horse sped Muhammad to Mount Moriah in Jerusalem. At the Rock of Abraham, the prophet met the Angel Gabriel, who escorted him to Heaven. Muhammad spoke all night with God, who commanded him to return to Earth with his sacred words. Muhammad returned and founded the Islamic religion. Over time, Islam gathered a vast body of followers from the Mediterranean through much of Asia.

After Muhammad's death, Muslims conquered the Byzantine Empire. In Jerusalem, a Muslim ruler, or caliph, built the Dome of the Rock on Temple Mount in 691. The Dome of the Rock is an imperial monument by which new Arab rulers asserted the truth of their religion. According to legend, the large rock under the dome is the place from which Muhammad ascended to Heaven.

During the eleventh century, travelers from western Europe visited the Holy Land to see the places where Jesus lived and died. They were

A miniature depicting Muhammad (on horseback), the prophet who founded the Islamic religion

al-Buraq (AHL-BUH-ROK)
caliph (KAY-LUFF)

shocked to find these holy places in the hands of the Muslims. In Germany, France, and England, armies gathered to capture the Holy Land. These expeditions, or Crusades, led to bloody fighting in the streets of Jerusalem. Several times, the Europeans conquered the city, only to lose it to the Muslims once again.

In 1516, Jerusalem fell to the Turkish-based Ottoman Empire. It remained a Muslim city for the next four centuries. Then in 1917, World War I brought Ottoman power to its knees. The British took over Jerusalem and the surrounding land, known by then as Palestine. Prodded by a growing movement called Zionism, the British issued a document known as the Balfour Declaration. The Balfour Declaration stated that Palestine should become a homeland for the Jewish people of the world.

In 1917, the British took over Jerusalem and the area surrounding it and decided that it should become a homeland for the Jewish people of the world.

CONTESTED SOIL

The Zionist movement arose among Jews in the nineteenth century and gained momentum in the decades that followed. The Zionists were largely secular socialists, and they were initially criticized by some Orthodox Jewish leaders. Zionists argued that the Jews were a displaced people, driven from their homeland by the Arabs and Christians. Wherever they went over the centuries, Jews had been persecuted. They should be given a land of their own where they could live and worship in safety.

Jewish people in Europe suffered unimaginable horrors under the German dictator Adolf Hitler, who rose to power in 1933.

Germany was defeated in 1945 at the end of World War II. As the truth about Hitler's atrocities came to light, the world looked upon Zionism with greater sympathy. In 1948, the newly established United Nations (UN) created the nation of Israel by dividing Palestine between the Arabs and the Jews. The UN determined that Jerusalem would be an international city, the first in the world. It would not be governed by any one country, but by the UN itself. Jerusalem would be a shrine to peace and religious freedom, welcoming people of all faiths.

Above: German dictator Adolf Hitler

Right: Israelis celebrate the first day of the new Jewish state.

The UN plan was doomed from the start. Palestinian Arabs felt they had not been considered when the plan was formed. Now, they were forced to leave land where they had lived and worked for countless generations. Fighting broke out as soon as the British withdrew in May 1948. Arab armies attacked Israel and seized East Jerusalem. Israeli troops finally halted the Arab forces as they pushed westward. By fall, the Arab nation of Jordan held East Jerusalem, while West Jerusalem lay in Israeli hands.

In the City of Peace, two hostile nations glared at one another across a boundary of land mines and barbed-wire fences. Arabs resented Israel's occupation of West Jerusalem and the rest of Israel. Israelis mourned the loss of the Temple Mount and other holy sites in Jordanian East Jerusalem. Despite the UN agreement that Jerusalem should be an international city, Israel claimed West Jerusalem as its national capital.

Jewish boys and girls dance the hora after the flag of Israel is raised to signal the birth of the new nation.

After nineteen years of bitterness and bloody skirmishes, Israel launched an all-out attack on Jordan in June 1967. Israeli tanks surrounded the Old City within East Jerusalem. Jordan pounded West Jerusalem with heavy artillery. After three days of street fighting, Israel captured East Jerusalem and merged the divided city into one. Jews rushed to the Temple Mount and prayed in thanksgiving at the Western Wall.

Following the 1967 conflict (known as the Six-Day War), the barbed wire came down and the land mines disappeared. Arabs and Jews were free to travel throughout the city. Yet the deep divisions that wracked the entire Middle East region were reflected in Jerusalem. Arabs resented the take-over of East Jerusalem by the Israelis. Many felt that a nation should be established for the Arabs who were driven from their homes when Israel was created. They wanted Jerusalem to become the capital of the nation of Palestine. Israelis lived in constant fear of an Arab uprising. To secure their hold on East Jerusalem, they established Jewish settlements in many of its neighborhoods and in

Mahdi Abdul Hadi
(MAH-H-DEE AHB-DOOL HAH-DEE)

Syrians who lost their homes during the 1967 Six-Day War gather around a radio in 1999 to hear that peace talks between Syria and Israel were to resume.

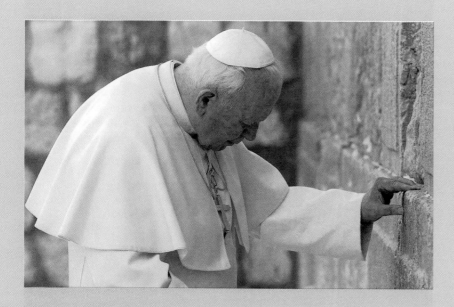

A Visit from the Pope

For the first time in 2,000 years, the leader of the Roman Catholic Church visited Jerusalem in March 2000. Christians, Jews, and Arabs gathered to hear Pope John Paul II speak about peace and redemption. Thousands flocked to hear the pope hold Mass at the Church of the Holy Sepulchre.

nearby villages. Arab groups, including the Palestine Liberation Organization (PLO), fought back. At times, both sides resorted to terrorist tactics.

In September 1993, Israeli and Palestinian leaders began the slow, painful process of peace negotiations. They hoped somehow to resolve the conflict that had surged around Israel for more than fifty years. They would search out a way to govern Jerusalem that would satisfy Arabs, Jews, and Christians alike.

Will it ever be possible to heal this wounded city, to bring its people together in unity and peace? "I'm pessimistic. You have to be," says Mahdi Abdul Hadi, a Palestinian who studies international affairs. "There is no solution for Jerusalem. It's an endless conflict."

Yet, some of Jerusalem's people find reason for hope. "We have to try everything in this city to make people get along," says former mayor Teddy Kollek. "[About] 300,000 people have visited [the city zoo] each year—ultra-religious, freethinkers, Arabs, Jews, all mixing. All through the summer, I saw children jump into a beautiful large fountain in one of the city parks—Arab children, Jewish children, their mothers standing next to each other rubbing shoulders." Kollek concludes, "It works."

A doll from Jerusalem

CELEBRATIONS!

On any day of the year, hotels in Jerusalem are packed. Camera-toting visitors crowd the streets, eager to catch a glimpse of the city's most famous sights. In the spring, more visitors than ever flood the city. They come to attend the annual Israeli Festival, a glorious medley of opera, music, dance, and theater from around the world. The Israeli Festival is one of the many celebrations held in Jerusalem. Some celebrations are cultural events, and others have spiritual meaning. All bring people together to marvel and to share.

EATING TO LIVE, LIVING TO EAT

Food is part of every celebration in Jerusalem, from graduation ceremonies to the most solemn religious holidays. On Friday mornings, shoppers throng the Mahneh Yehudah Market on Jerusalem's Jaffa Street. They walk from stall to stall, haggling with vendors over the price of melons, figs, eggplants, and lamb. On Fridays, Jerusalem's Jewish families prepare for the Sabbath dinner to be served that evening after sundown. Throughout the city's Jewish neighborhoods, food is on everyone's mind.

With its mountainous terrain and sparse rainfall, the land around Jerusalem is not kind to the farmer. But with careful irrigation, farmers raise generous crops. Though there are no grazing lands for beef cattle, the mountain grasses support healthy flocks of sheep and goats. Lamb and kid are used in many dishes served in Jerusalem's homes and restaurants. Chicken and eggs are also plentiful.

Visitors may be startled by the typical breakfast in Jerusalem. Instead of heaping mounds of pancakes and bacon, the people of Jerusalem serve up a lush green salad, garnished with cucumbers and slices of fruit. Breakfast, like most meals, comes with a steaming pot of strong Israeli coffee.

The people of Jerusalem eat their main meal in the evening. Along with salad, meat, and vegetable dishes they serve crisp loaves of *challah*. Challah is a bread made with strips of dough. The dough is braided to form a twisted pattern when baked.

A Jewish boy eating felafel

Mahneh Yehudah (MAH-NEH YEY-HOO-DAH)
Jaffa (JAFF-UH)
challah (<u>H</u>AH-LAH)
za-ata (ZAH-AH-TAH)
felafel (FAH-LAH-FELL)
souk (SOOK)

A spice merchant in Old Jerusalem

People in Jerusalem love pastries of all kinds. Many mouth-watering treats are sold from stands on the streets. One favorite is a deep-fried doughnut filled with sesame paste. Dip it in *za-ata*, a delicious mixture of sweet spices and sunflower seeds. *Felafel* is a fried chick pea mixture wrapped in pita bread.

Open-air Arab markets are known as *souks*. Stalls in the souk sell *sachlad*, a frothy concoction of hot milk topped with raisins, cinnamon, and ground nuts. Arab children enjoy a mug of sachlad much as American kids love to stop for an ice-cream cone.

This Jewish Sabbath dinner includes brisket, knishes, and challah.

A PASSION FOR THE ARTS

Literature is another form of expression for the people of Jerusalem. Bookstores overflow with western bestsellers as well as offerings by Israeli writers. Some of the finest novels and poetry convey the anguish of the Arab–Israeli conflict. In his 1985 novel *Arabesque*, Christian Arab Anton Shams writes in Hebrew about the Jewish state and the displaced Arab Palestinians. Novelist Amos Oz describes the bloodshed and uncertainty of the struggle in his novel *Michael*. Palestinian Arab poetry celebrates weddings and other joyous occasions. It is also a form of protest against Israeli oppression of the Arab people.

Galleries in the East Jerusalem neighborhood of Mishkenot Sha'Ananim display the work of local painters and sculptors. Sometimes artists set up their easels outdoors and paint quick portraits of passersby. More successful artists and writers live in the nearby neighborhood called Yemin Moshe. Rents here are among the steepest in the city.

Music and dance are knit tightly into the fabric of Jerusalem life. Popular music draws upon ancient Middle Eastern rhythms and melodies, blending them with an electric modern beat. Young people dance to both Israeli and western hits. On cool summer evenings, rock bands give outdoor concerts at Sultan's Pool and other parks. Jazz is also popular. Jazz fans enjoy vocal and instrumental performances at the Pargod Theater.

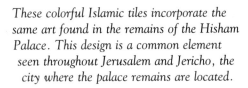

These colorful Islamic tiles incorporate the same art found in the remains of the Hisham Palace. This design is a common element seen throughout Jerusalem and Jericho, the city where the palace remains are located.

Mishkenot Sha'Ananim (MEESH-KEH-NOHT SHAH-AH-NAH-NEEM)
Yemin Moshe (YEH-MEEN MOH-SHAY)

A view of Jerusalem's Yemin Moshe neighborhood

For those who prefer the classics, the Jerusalem Symphony Orchestra gives concerts at Henry Crown Symphony Hall, or at the Binyanei Ha-Uma Concert Hall. Outdoor performances of operas and orchestral pieces are featured at spring festivals. Breathtaking sacred music shimmers beneath the vaulted ceilings of Jerusalem's churches. During the Christmas and Easter seasons, many churches feature special concert programs.

Folk dancers in Jerusalem

FESTIVALS AND FAITH

In Jerusalem, religion can determine where people live, what they wear, and even what foods they eat. Not surprisingly, religion also decides which holidays people celebrate. Jews, Christians, and Muslims each follow their own traditions. The holidays of each faith are filled with beauty, sorrow, and joy.

Right: Pilgrims praying at the Western Wall

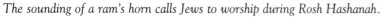
The sounding of a ram's horn calls Jews to worship during Rosh Hashanah.

According to the Jewish calendar, the New Year begins in September. In Jerusalem, the Jewish New Year, Rosh Hashanah, is a solemn two-day celebration. The ringing notes of a ram's horn, or *shofar*, call thousands of Jews to their synagogues for worship. Ten days later, Jews celebrate Yom Kippur, or the Day of Atonement. Yom Kippur is considered the most sacred day of the year. Jews attend services, repent of their sins, and ask forgiveness from God and from anyone they may have wronged in the preceding year. They begin the New Year purified and restored.

Sukkot is a lively Jewish holiday to celebrate the autumn harvest. It is the favorite holiday for many Jerusalem children. The streets fill with dancers, jugglers, and musicians. Each family sets up a temporary hut where everyone lives for seven days. It is like going away for vacation in your own backyard.

Celebrated in December, Hanukkah is an eight-day festival to commemorate the miracle of the lamp oil at the Second Temple. Passover, a seven-day festival in March or April, recalls the flight of the ancient Israelites who had been held as slaves in Egypt. For seven nights, Jewish families gather for ceremonial dinners called *seders*. Through readings, songs, special foods, and recited questions and answers, the seder re-creates the Biblical story.

Seven weeks after Passover, thousands of Jews flock to the Western Wall for the Feast of Weeks, or Shavuot. At dawn they lift their prayers to the skies. Shavuot begins a three-week period of mourning for the temple that was destroyed in A.D. 70.

A Jewish shofar made from the horn of a ram.

Rosh Hashanah (ROASH HAH-SHAH-NAH)
shofar (SHOH-FAR)
Yom Kippur (YOHM KEE-POOR)
Sukkot (SOO-COAT)
seder (SEH-DAYR)
Shavuot (SHAH-VOO-OHT)

A carved wooden statue of the infant Jesus

Christmas and Easter are the most important holidays in the Christian calendar. Both have their roots in and around Jerusalem. Each Christmas, thousands of Christians visit the town of Bethlehem, the birthplace of Jesus Christ. Pilgrims pray at the Church of the Nativity, thought to stand on the site where Christ was born.

The Church of the Holy Sepulchre in Jerusalem is the focus of celebration during the Easter season. Carrying palm branches, devout Christians walk in procession along the Via Dolorosa, or Road of Sorrows, believed to be the route Christ took from the Mount of Olives to his crucifixion at Calvary. Holy Sepulchre marks the site where Christ is believed to have died and risen from his tomb.

During Ramadan, the ninth month in the Islamic calendar, about 200,000 Muslims pray each day at the Dome of the Rock. For Muslims, Ramadan is the holiest time of the year. It celebrates God's gift of the Koran to the prophet Muhammad, and thus to Muslims throughout the world. Like the Jewish Yom Kippur, Ramadan is a time of atonement. Muslims ask forgiveness for their sins from God and humanity. From dawn until sunset each day throughout the month, Muslims neither eat nor drink.

Fasting during Ramadan is seen as a way to purify the body and the spirit, and to honor the teachings of the Koran.

At the end of the month they enjoy a great feast and give gifts to the poor.

Muslims celebrate the birth of the Prophet Muhammad on the twelfth day of the third Islamic calendar month. Traditional Muslims observe this holiday by reciting poetry in praise of Muhammad and his teachings. Another important holiday is the Night of the Ascension, usually between the twenty-sixth and twenty-seventh days of the seventh month. Activities commemorate Muhammad's mystical journey to Jerusalem and his ascension to paradise.

Nuns praying at the Western Wall on Palm Sunday

Via Dolorosa (VEE-ah doh-loh-ROH-sah)
Ramadan (RAH-mah-don)

The Fourth Station of the Cross along the Via Dolorosa marks the place where Jesus met Mary.

Stations of the Cross

According to Christian tradition, Christ carried his own cross to Calvary, pausing fourteen times to rest along the way. Led by Roman Catholic priests, Christians retrace Christ's final journey every Friday throughout the year. The procession begins at St. Stephen's Church, the first of the Fourteen Stations of the Cross. The pilgrims stop to pray at each of the stations on their way to Holy Sepulchre Church (left).

BEAUTY

The Talmud is a set of sacred laws and commentaries gathered by Jewish sages early in the Christian era. One passage in the Talmud says that God handed ten measures of beauty to the world. He bestowed nine of the ten upon the city of Jerusalem.

Nestled among the mountains, its pink and cream-colored buildings clinging to the hillsides, Jerusalem is one of the loveliest cities on earth. Despite the strife that tears it apart, it welcomes visitors with its Middle Eastern charm. Jerusalem is full of history and tradition. Each neighborhood has its own treasures to reveal.

Talmud (TAHL-MOOD)

THE MODERN WEST

West Jerusalem is the most modern part of the city. Its broad streets and shopping malls are modeled on those in Europe and the United States. Yet West Jerusalem's buildings have a Middle Eastern flair. The YMCA is one of the most remarkable landmarks in this part of the city. The Jerusalem Y was built in the 1930s by the same architectural firm that designed New York's Empire State Building. In keeping with the buildings around it, the Y uses Byzantine and Islamic elements. From the observation deck on the top story, 152 feet (46 m) above the sidewalk, visitors have a spectacular view. The YMCA has the only carillon, or set of melodic bells, in the Middle East.

According to legend, the wood for Jesus' cross came from a valley in West Jerusalem. The Monastery of the Cross, now a Greek Orthodox Church, recalls this long-standing belief. On a nearby hilltop stands Israel's Parliament building, the

Jerusalem's YMCA building

Knesset. The beautiful menorah in front of the Knesset is engraved with scenes from Jewish history. The lobby displays a mosaic by artist Marc Chagall. Though security is tight, visitors are welcome to watch the Knesset in session. The adjoining Wohl Rose Park is often the site of diplomatic receptions.

Not far from the Knesset stands the Israel Museum, opened in 1965. The museum is a celebration of Israel's art and history. On display are Jewish and Islamic paintings, as well as works by some of the finest European artists of the nineteenth century. Artifacts and pictures trace four thousand years of Israeli history and culture. The jewel of the museum is the Shrine of the Book, which houses many of the priceless Dead Sea Scrolls. Also on exhibit are a series of letters written by Judean General Simmon Bar-Cochva, who led an uprising against the Romans in A.D. 132.

The Shepherd's Discovery

One day in 1947, a Palestinian shepherd discovered a pile of parchment scrolls hidden in the Caves of Qumran outside Jerusalem. The scrolls proved to be ancient copies of Biblical texts, including the complete Book of Isaiah from the Old Testament. The Dead Sea Scrolls, as they are known, are among the most important archaeological finds of the twentieth century.

The Caves of Qumran

Knesset (K-NESS-ETT)
Simmon Bar-Cochva
(SHEE-MOHN BAR KO<u>H</u>-BAH)
Qumran (KOOM-RON)

The neighborhood called Me'a She'arim stands in sharp contrast to the modern sections of West Jerusalem. Me'a She'arim is controlled by Ultra-Orthodox Jews who live strictly by Talmudic law. The neighborhood was founded in 1874 as a walled fortress by Jewish immigrants from Lithuania. Extreme modesty is a requirement in Me'a She'arim. Visitors must dress discreetly at all times, and men and women may not hold hands in public. On the Sabbath, no one is permitted to drive a car. Zealous residents sometimes spit upon or even hurl stones at visitors who dare to break these rules.

A family in Independence Park, the largest park in Jerusalem

Me'a She'arim (MAY-AH SHEH-AH-REEM)

The most famous landmark in the Yemin Moshe neighborhood is the old windmill that stands above the quiet streets. A museum at the windmill's base recalls the life of Moses Montifiore, an English Jew who established this neighborhood in the 1850s. Montifiore created Yemin Moshe as a refuge for impoverished Jews from the Old City. Today, it is one of Jerusalem's most elegant sections.

Yemin Moshe's Liberty Bell Park is one of the more unusual parks in Jerusalem. Its centerpiece is an exact replica of the Liberty Bell in Philadelphia, a symbol of U.S. independence from Great Britain. Inscribed on both bells is a verse from the Biblical Book of Isaiah. These words proclaimed American independence in 1776 and Israeli independence in 1948: "Proclaim liberty throughout the land, and to all the inhabitants thereof."

Independence Park is the largest public park in the city. According to legend, a kind-hearted lion

A young girl sitting on the Fountain of the Lions in a Jerusalem park

An Arab boy

once guarded a cave at this spot. The lion protected the bodies of religious martyrs, whether they were Jews, Christians, or Muslims. Another important park is Zion Square in the heart of the business district. The square is a meeting place for friends and couples. Zionists rallied here in 1947 and 1948 to call for Israel to become an independent nation.

OUTSIDE THE GATES

The oldest part of Jerusalem, the Old City, is ringed with high stone walls. People enter and leave the Old City through a series of gates. For hundreds of years, the land outside the gates was a wild desert, home to nomadic herders and warriors. During the nineteenth century, Jerusalem expanded into this area. Today's East Jerusalem includes these new sections in addition to the Old City.

In ancient times, most burials took place beyond the city walls. In 1863, a British archaeologist discovered a tomb outside the Damascus Gate that fit the description of Christ's tomb given in the Bible. Some people believe that the Garden Tomb, as it is called, was the site of Christ's burial, not the tomb at the Church of the Holy Sepulchre.

The Garden Tomb

The white stone Rockefeller Museum, near Herod's Gate, houses artifacts from ancient times as well as documents, pictures, furnishings, and art from Israel's historic periods. Exhibits include Egyptian antiques, wood panels from mosques, and several of the Dead Sea Scrolls.

Tradition holds that the stone to build King Solomon's Temple came from a quarry in present-day East Jerusalem. Visitors to Zedekiah's Cave can see where blocks of stone were carved away for use in construction. Some records claim that tunnels from the cave once led all the way to the Sinai Peninsula in

A young Israeli girl with ten-day-old kittens

present-day Egypt. No one knows if this story is true. But tunnels do lead beneath the Old City. An adventurous visitor can follow these underground pathways, walking in the footsteps of soldiers and refugees who lived two thousand years ago.

According to the Bible, Jesus climbed the Mount of Olives on the evening of the Last Supper before the Crucifixion. Today, the Mount of Olives is a lively Muslim neighborhood with many mosques and souks. Jews, Christians, and Muslims are buried in the cemetery here, which has sections for each of the three faiths.

The Rockefeller Museum was designed by architect Austin Harrison.

WITHIN THE WALLS

When American writer Mark Twain visited Jerusalem, he was amazed by the compactness of the Old City. "You can walk entirely around the city in an hour," he wrote. "I do not know how else to make one understand how small it is." The walls surrounding the Old City are about 40 feet (12 m) high and 2.5 miles (4 km) in circumference. Most of the walls that survive were built in the 1500s by the Ottoman Turks, though some sections are much older. Flights of stone steps lead to the Rampart Walk along the top of the wall, providing an excellent view of the buildings and streets below.

A young Jewish boy

The Cardo, a long-buried road that dates to Roman times, is now an underground mall lined with Roman pillars.

Jerusalem's holy places and historic landmarks are densely concentrated in the Old City. Four distinct neighborhoods lie within the walls: the Jewish, Christian, Muslim, and Armenian Quarters. The Jewish Quarter is the Old City's most affluent section. Jews were not allowed to live here under Jordanian rule, but after 1967 they returned and restored hundreds of old houses. The Jewish Quarter Museum traces the history of the quarter from 1948 to current times. A multi-media presentation dramatizes the 1948 war and the Six-Day War of 1967.

Early in the 1980s, archaeologists discovered traces of a long-buried road beneath 13 feet (4 m) of rubble in the Jewish Quarter. The road, known as the Cardo, appeared on ancient maps and dated back to Roman times.

The Cardo is now an underground mall lined with shops and restaurants. Original Roman pillars mark the course it followed two thousand years ago.

The highlight of the Christian Quarter is the Church of the Holy Sepulchre, built by Crusaders in the twelfth century. The present church stands on the site where Queen Helena found a tomb and three buried crosses. The church is controlled by six Christian denominations today. In an annual ceremony on the night

before Easter, flames of "holy fire" burst forth from the tomb where believers claim Christ was laid to rest. Eastern Orthodox priests light the holy fire to symbolize Christ's suffering and the redemption of the world.

The Bible recounts that Christ walked in a garden called Gethsemane on the night of the Last Supper. Some of the olive trees in present-day

Gethsemane were planted in Roman times. Nearby is a cave thought to contain the graves of Mary, Joseph, and Mary's parents.

A beautiful notecard from Jerusalem with real flowers from the Holy Land

The smallest and quietest neighborhood in the Old City is the Armenian Quarter. Between 1915 and 1918, the Armenians suffered genocide at the hands of the Turks. Thousands of refugees fled to Jerusalem. The Armenian Museum tells the story of the genocide and the growth of Jerusalem's Armenian colony. At the annual Feast of St. James, the leader of the Armenian community sits on the throne of St. James the Lesser in the ornate St. James Cathedral.

Leading into the Muslim Quarter is the splendid Damascus Gate. The gate is a meeting place for Arabs in the Old City. At its base splashes the Sabil, the re-creation of an ancient fountain.

The Muslim Quarter borders on the Temple Mount, the most sacred corner of this holy city. To the Muslims, the Temple Mount is al-Haram al-Sharif, "the Noble Sanctuary." Here stands Al-Aqsa, the most important mosque in Jerusalem. It is an impressive building with a silver dome, probably constructed in the eighth century. Though the inside is plain, the floors are decorated with beautiful Persian rugs. Visitors must remove their shoes before they enter.

No site is more sacred to people of the Jewish faith than the Western Wall on the Temple Mount. About 160 feet (49 m) in length, the wall is all that remains of the Second Temple, which was destroyed by the Romans in A.D. 70. It is sometimes called the Wailing Wall because Jews wept there over the temple's destruction. According to legend, the wall itself sometimes

The Damascus Gate

An Armenian man

54

The Dome of the Rock

weeps. Every day, thousands of Jews pray at the wall, men and women going to separate sections for this purpose. People write prayers on slips of paper and press them between the wall's massive stones. Like mortar, these paper prayers fill every crack and crevice.

For Muslims, the Dome of the Rock is the most revered holy place in Jerusalem. The dome covers the rock from which, Muslims believe, the prophet Muhammad rose on his journey to heaven. On this rock, it is also said, the prophet Abraham prepared to sacrifice his son to God. Whether they are Jews, Christians, or Muslims, all who climb the steps to this historic spot are touched by its power, and by the beauty and wonder of the city of Jerusalem.

al-Haram al-Sharif
(EHL-HAH-ROM EHL-SHAH-REEF)

FAMOUS LANDMARKS

Yad Vashem

The Western Wall

Church of the Holy Sepulchre
Built by Crusaders in the 1140s, this church stands on the site where some believe Christ died. Weekly processions trace Jesus' route from the Mount of Olives, along the Via Dolorosa, to the Church of the Holy Sepulchre on the Hill of Calvary. The church is controlled by six Christian denominations.

Dome of the Rock
This monumental building was completed by a Muslim caliph in 691. The dome covers the Rock of Abraham, from which Muslims believe the prophet Muhammad rose to heaven.

Western Wall
After the destruction of the Second Temple in A.D. 70, only this wall remained. It is a symbol and a holy site for people of the Jewish faith.

Tower of David
This tower stands on the fortified hill known as the Citadel. The tower may be a remnant of King Herod's palace built here around the time of Christ. It has served as the Museum of Jerusalem since 1957.

Armenian Museum
At the heart of the Armenian Quarter, this museum presents the tragic story of this people's genocide under the Ottoman Turks. It also shows the formation of the Armenian community in Jerusalem.

Old Yishuv Court Museum
The history of the Jewish Quarter comes to life through pictures and artifacts at this museum. Exhibits cover the cultures of Sephardic, Ashkenazi, and Oriental Jews.

The Cardo
In the early 1980s, archaeologists discovered an ancient road hidden beneath 13 feet (4 m) of rubble. This Roman thoroughfare, the Cardo, is now an underground shopping mall lined with Roman pillars.

War of Independence Memorial
Located in the Jewish Quarter, this monument commemorates the war of 1948 when Israel became a nation. An electronic map of Jerusalem shows the streets and houses where fighting took place.

Ramban Synagogue
Still fully in use, this is the oldest synagogue in Jerusalem. Across its courtyard are several yeshivas, schools where students study Jewish culture and law.

The Church of Mary Magdalene
on the Mount of Olives

Temple Mount and
Al-Aqsa Mosque

The Tower of David

Hasmonean Tunnel

This ancient passageway reaches deep beneath the Muslim Quarter. It leads from the Western Wall to the Via Dolorosa. Much of the tunnel is now open to the public.

Nebi Samuel

This is one of many Arab villages that are part of East Jerusalem. The mosque marks the possible burial place of the prophet Samuel. Samuel is honored by both Muslims and Jews.

Knesset

Though the official capital of Israel is Tel Aviv, this low, wide building in West Jerusalem is the seat of the Israeli government. Visitors can watch the Knesset in session and admire the splendid artwork that adorns the building.

Israel Museum

Opened in 1965, this museum covers both art and history. One annex, the Shrine of the Book, houses several of the priceless Dead Sea Scrolls.

Yad Vashem

This museum is a tribute to the millions who died in the Holocaust, the destruction of Jews and others under Adolf Hitler. The sculpted Wall of the Holocaust and Heroism depicts the Holocaust and the formation of the nation of Israel.

Al-Aqsa Mosque

The most important mosque in Jerusalem, Al-Aqsa shares the Temple Mount with other Jewish and Islamic shrines. It was probably built by a Muslim caliph in the eighth century. The floors are covered with beautiful Persian rugs.

Mount of Olives

According to the Bible, Christ climbed this hill on the evening before his crucifixion. Today, it is a Muslim neighborhood with a cemetery that has Muslim, Christian, and Jewish sections.

Bethlehem

Only 6 miles (10 km) south of Jerusalem, this small city now lies in Palestinian territory. Christians honor Bethlehem as the birthplace of Jesus Christ. The Church of the Nativity in Manger Square was built in the fourth century A.D. It is thought to stand on the site where Jesus was born.

FAST FACTS

POPULATION   567,100

AREA   41 square miles (106 sq km)

ALTITUDE   2,400 feet (732 m)

LOCATION   Jerusalem is located in central Israel on the border of Jordan. To the south lies the Dead Sea. The city is built on a series of hills and has mountains on three sides. Though not recognized by the United Nations, Jerusalem serves as Israel's capital city.

CLIMATE   Jerusalem has a warm, dry climate, with hot summers and mild winters. The average July temperature is 76 degrees Fahrenheit (24° Celsius). The average temperature in January is 55 degrees Fahrenheit (13° C). Jerusalem receives about 22 inches (56 centimeters) of precipitation per year.

ECONOMY   Factories in Jerusalem produce plastics, chemicals, clothing, machinery, and leather goods. The city is known for many crafts including silverwork, diamond polishing, pottery, and woodwork. Tourism is also a major industry.

CHRONOLOGY

2000 B.C.
Nomadic tribes occupy the land where Jerusalem now stands.

1500 B.C.
Jewish tribes enter the area and make it their home.

1000 B.C.
King David unites the Jewish tribes and makes Jerusalem their capital.

953 B.C.
King Solomon, David's son, completes a temple on Mount Moriah.

586 B.C.
Jerusalem is conquered by the Babylonians; Solomon's temple is destroyed.

515 B.C.
The Second Temple is completed with the help of the Persians.

186 B.C.
Syrians turn the Second Temple into a shrine to the Greek god Zeus.

154 B.C.
Jews recapture the temple, giving rise to the Hanukkah holiday.

Beginning of the Christian calendar
Jesus Christ is born in the nearby town of Bethlehem.

A.D. 33
Jesus is crucified by Pontius Pilate, the Roman governor of Judea.

70
The Romans destroy the Second Temple, leaving only its western wall.

326
Roman Queen Helena visits Jerusalem and finds the possible tomb of Christ; Roman Emperor Constantine orders a church built on the spot.

*Palestinian children
in Jerusalem*

*Schoolchildren near
the Damascus Gate*

c. 570
Muslim prophet Muhammad is
born in Arabia.

691
Muslim caliph builds the Dome
of the Rock on the Temple
Mount.

1100s to 1300s
Europeans launch a series of
Crusades to capture the Holy
Land from the Muslims.

1516
Jerusalem is taken over by the
Ottoman Empire.

1917
British take over Palestine and
issue the Balfour Declaration,
calling for a Jewish homeland.

1948
The United Nations creates the
nation of Israel, unleashing war
between Arabs and Jews;
Jerusalem is divided between
Israel and Jordan.

1967
In the Six-Day War, Israel
captures East Jerusalem and
unites the city.

1993
Arabs and Israelis begin peace
negotiations at Oslo, Norway.

1996
Riots break out when Israel
opens the north entrance to the
Hasmonean Tunnel.

2000
Pope John Paul II visits
Jerusalem and says Mass at the
Church of the Holy Sepulchre.

JERUSALEM

A B C D E F G H I J K

1 Binyanei Ha-Uma Concert Hall · War of Independence Memorial · ME'A SHE'ARIM

2 Mahane Yehuda Market · Garden Tomb · Herod's Gate · Rockefeller Museum

Zedekiah's Cave · MUSLIM QUARTER · Gethsemane

3 Pargod Theater · Jaffa Street · Damascus Gate · East Jerusalem · Via Dolorosa · St. Stephen's Church

West Jerusalem · CHRISTIAN QUARTER · Dome of the Rock · Temple Mount

4 Wohl Rose Park · Independence Park · Church of the Holy Sepulchre · Hasmonean Tunnel

OLD CITY · Tower of David · Cardo · Western Wall

5 Knesset · Rampart Walk · ARMENIAN QUARTER · JEWISH QUARTER · El-Aqsa Mosque

YMCA · Sultan's Pool · YEMIN MOSHE · St. James Cathedral · Ramban Synagogue · Gihon Springs

6 Israel Museum · Monastery of the Cross · Henry Crown Symphony Hall · Liberty Bell Park · Mishkenot Sha'Ananim · Armenian Museum

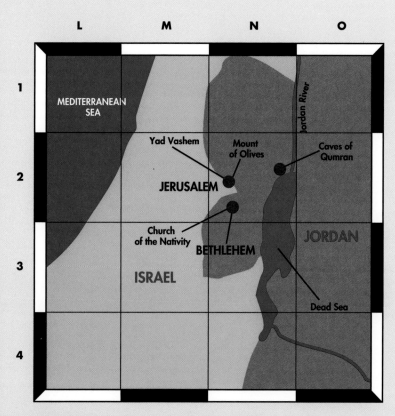

JERUSALEM & SURROUNDINGS

GLOSSARY

affluent: Wealthy

artifact: Relic, object from the past

atrocity: Cruel, horrible act

bestow: Present as a gift

candelabra: Holder with places for several candles

carillon: Set of bells designed to play melodies

compact: Small, contained

cornerstone: Foundation stone

cuisine: Style of cooking

emigrate: Settle in another country

facade: Front

genocide: Large-scale killing intended to wipe out an ethnic group

irony: Surprising twist

martyr: Person who dies for his or her beliefs

mosque: Muslim house of worship, usually having a dome on top

parchment: Sturdy paperlike substance made from cloth or tree bark

patriarch: Father of a community

pilgrim: Person who makes a journey for religious purposes

prophet: Person who speaks for God

refuge: Place of safety

scroll: Roll of paper or parchment

synagogue: Jewish house of worship

tablet: Sheet of clay or metal on which messages are written

zealous: Driven by a passionate belief

Picture Identifications

Cover: Dome of the Rock on Temple Mount; a young Israeli girl
Page 1: A young Israeli boy
Pages 4–5: Dome of the Rock on Temple Mount
Pages 8–9: Arab women and children visiting Mount Olive
Pages 20–21: A Sephardic family celebrating the Jewish festival of Passover by sharing a picnic in West Jerusalem
Pages 34–35: Israeli teenager in Jerusalem
Pages 44–45: Wohl Rose Park, next to the Knesset

INDEX

TO FIND OUT MORE

BOOKS

Brown, Stephen F. *Christianity*. World Religions series. New York: Facts on File, 1991.

Hintz, Martin, and Stephen Hintz. *Israel*. Enchantment of the World Second Series. Danbury, Conn.: Children's Press, 1999.

Humphreys, Andrew. *Jerusalem*. *A Lonely Planet City Guide*. Hawthorn, Australia: Lonely Planet Publications, 1997.

Jerusalem & the Holy Land. Dorling Kindersley Travel Guides. New York: Dorling Kindersley Publishing, Inc. 2000.

Morrison, Martha, and Stephen F. Brown. *Judaism*. World Religions series. New York: Facts on File, 1991.

Nellhaus, Arlynn. *The Heart of Jerusalem: A Traveler's Guide to Visits, Celebrations, and Sojourns*. Santa Fe, New Mexico: John Muir Publications, 1999.

Paris, Alan. *Jerusalem 3000: Kids Discover the City of Gold*. New York: Pitspopany Press, 1995.

Pearlman, Moshe, and Yaacov Yannai. *Historical Sites in the Holy Land*. Valley Forge, Penn.: Judson Press, 1985.

Pirotta, Saviour. *Jerusalem*. Holy Cities series. New York: Dillon Press, 1993.

Ross, Stewart. *Causes and Consequences of the Arab-Israeli Conflict*. Austin, Texas: Raintree Steck-Vaughn, 1996.

Tames, Richard. *Muslims*. Beliefs and Cultures series. Danbury, Conn.: Children's Press, 1996.

Zanger, Walter. *Jerusalem*. Great Cities series. New York: Blackbirch Press, 1991.

ONLINE SITES

Infotour: Israeli Tourism & Recreation
http://www.tourism.yellowpages.co.il/yp/yp.cgi
This site has a link to Jerusalem and the region with information on attractions, museums, art galleries, national parks, things to do, things for children to do, places to stay, a calendar of events, shopping, entertainment, restaurants, tours, and current exhibits.

Israel Museum
http://www.imj.org.il/
This guide to the Israel Museum campus has information on guided tours and links to the several museums including the Dead Sea Scrolls-Shrine of the Book, the Bronfman Biblical and Archaeological Museum, Judaica and Jewish Ethnography Wing, the Fine Arts Wing, the Billy Rose Art Garden, and the Ruth Youth Wing. Each link has pictures and extensive commentary on the current exhibits.

Israel Tourist
http://www.israel-tourist-information.com/
Features sightseeing, history, accommodations, a Jerusalem travel guide, links to many attractions including the Dome of the Rock, the Old City, the Via Dolorosa, accommodations, activities, events, travel information, maps, and more.

Jerusalem: City of Gold
http://www.jerusalemtourist.com/
Includes pictures and information on Jerusalem attractions, museums, sports, shopping, hotels, and restaurants; a detailed map of the city; Hebrew for tourists; travel tips, and much more.

ABOUT THE AUTHOR

Deborah Kent grew up in Little Falls, New Jersey, and received a B.A. in English from Oberlin College. She earned a master's degree from Smith College School for Social Work. After working for four years at the University Settlement House in New York City, she moved to San Miguel de Allende in central Mexico. There she wrote her first young-adult novel, *Belonging*. Ms. Kent is the author of many titles in the Children's Press Cities of the World series. She lives in Chicago with her husband, author R. Conrad Stein, and their daughter Janna.